DINOSAURS!

tiger tales

5 River Road, Suite 128, Wilton, CT 06897
Published in the United States 2022
Text by Lauren Crisp
Photographic images courtesy of www.shutterstock.co.uk
Text and illustrations copyright © 2022 Little Tiger Press Ltd.
ISBN-13: 978-1-6643-4036-7
ISBN-10: 1-6643-4036-X
Printed in China
LTK/2700/1099/0122

www.tigertalesbooks.com

The world is an ever-changing place, and the
people within it are capable of incredible things:
discoveries are made, records are broken, new facts
are found, and history recovered. We will be happy
to revise and update information in future editions.

DINOSAURS!

tiger tales

WHAT ARE DINOSAURS?

Dinosaurs were **reptiles** that roamed the Earth millions of years ago, during the **Mesozoic era**.

The Mesozoic era (or period of time) lasted for around 186 million years!

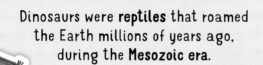

Dinosaurs lived on land, unlike the **pterosaurs** (flying reptiles) and **plesiosaurs** (swimming reptiles), which lived around the same time.

The Mesozoic era was split into three periods:

TRIASSIC: 252 to 201 million years ago (MYA)

JURASSIC: 201 to 145 MYA

CRETACEOUS: 145 to 66 MYA

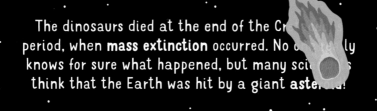

The dinosaurs died at the end of the Cr... period, when **mass extinction** occurred. No o... ...ly knows for sure what happened, but many sci... ...s think that the Earth was hit by a giant **aster...**

The dinosaurs disappeared, along with many other creatures, but some early **birds** survived, and it is believed that the birds we see today are a distant **relative of dinosaurs**.

Fossils are the remains or traces of very, very **old living things**, such as animals, plants, and insects. They are formed over **millions of years**, and it is very exciting when a new fossil is discovered—especially if it is a **dinosaur fossil**!

The dinosaurs lived many millions of years before human beings. So how do we know they existed? We know because of **fossils**.

Sometimes, a fossilized dinosaur **footprint**, also called an **ichnite**, is found—this means the dinosaur must have been stomping through thick, squishy mud, and its footprint turned into stone!

Dinosaurs lived all over the world!

The first dinosaur to ever be named was the **Megalosaurus** (MEG-uh-low-SORE-us) in 1824.

There were probably many thousands of different **species** of dinosaur, but only about 700 have been discovered and given a name so far.

DID YOU

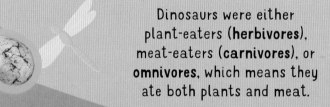

Dinosaurs were either plant-eaters (**herbivores**), meat-eaters (**carnivores**), or **omnivores**, which means they ate both plants and meat.

As far as the experts know, all dinosaurs laid **eggs**, and they probably either buried them or sat on them to keep them warm, just like birds do today.

The word **dinosaur** means "terrible lizard"!

New dinosaurs are always being discovered, and what we know about them is constantly **changing**! Will you be the next to **discover a dinosaur**?

A person who studies dinosaurs and their fossils is called a **paleontologist**.

KNOW?

Paleontologists discover a lot about dinosaurs through fossils:

They learn what a dinosaur ate by studying **coprolite**, or fossilized poop!

They can calculate how old a dinosaur was when it died by counting lines in the bone, just like counting tree rings.

They can figure out how big a dinosaur might have been from the size of its footprint.

HERRERASAURUS

Her-RARE-uh-SORE-us

PREDATOR AT LARGE

Herrerasaurus lived around 228 million years ago, making it one of the **earliest dinosaurs** to have roamed the Earth!

Sharp, serrated teeth for tearing flesh

Sharp claws for grasping prey

DISCOVERY

Year: 1959

Location: Argentina

By: Victorino Herrera, a goatherd

Name: Given in honor of its discoverer

It was very **speedy** and had great eyesight... perfect for catching prey!

HERRERASAURUS

Triassic

Jurassic

Prowling through the forest heat, this dino loved to eat **fresh meat!**

It was a **biped**, which means that it only used two legs for walking.

It is thought to have eaten small, mammal-like creatures called **synapsids. Kannemeyeria** (KAN-eh-mee-AIR-ee-uh) is an example of a synapsid.

Herrerasaurus ate meat, which made it a **carnivore**. It had a special jaw that allowed it to hold tightly onto its prey!

STATS

Period: Triassic (228 MYA)

Diet: Meat

Height: Around 5 ft (1.5 m)

Length: About 10–15 ft (3–4.5 m)

Weight: Around 500 lbs (220 kg)

Postosuchus (POH-stow-SOO-kus), which looked like an enormous crocodile, could definitely have given Herrerasaurus a hard time...and maybe even killed it!

Cretaceous

PLATEOSAURUS

PLAY-tee-uh-SORE-us

Plateosauru~~s~~ ~~herbivore. It~~ ~~ferns and lea~~ ~~using its~~ ~~plant~~

Ten bones in its neck made it bendy

Plateosaurus came in **different sizes**. It could grow pretty big if it found a lot of plants to eat!

DISCOVERY

Year: 1834

Location: Germany

By: Johann Friedrich Engelhart

Name: Means "broad lizard" due to its large frame

Short arms with sharp, grasping claws

Paleontologists have argued over how Plateosaurus moved around, but because of the position of its hands, it's likely that it walked on its two hind (back) feet, making it a **biped**.

PLATEOSAURUS

Triassic

Jurassic

This dino liked to walk around with both its front legs off the ground!

If Plateosaurus grew extremely large, it might have gotten **stuck in the mud** and died there.

This could be why so many (around 100!) well-preserved Plateosaurus fossilized **skeletons** have been found.

Walking on two legs allowed Plateosaurus to reach high into the trees to **snack on leaves.**

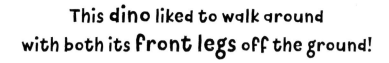

Strong back legs for running

STATS

Period: Triassic (210 MYA)

Diet: Plants

Height: Around 10 ft (3 m)

Length: Around 23-32 ft (7-10 m)

Weight: Up to around 8,800 lbs (4,000 kg)

STEGOSAURUS

STEG-uh-SORE-us

A small, long, narrow skull

Stegosaurus was an **armored** dinosaur with plates along its back.

The name **Stegosaurus** means "roof lizard" because when fossils were first found, it was thought that its plates laid flat, like shingles on a roof. That was until paleontologists discovered the plates actually pointed upright!

It had a deadly **spiked tail** that it could swing at predators.

DISCOVERY

Year: 1876

Location: United States

By: M.P. Felch / O.C. Marsh

Name: Means "roof lizard"

Triassic   Jurassic

Although this dino wasn't **bright**, its **tail** would help it win a **fight!**

Around 17 diamond-shaped plates along its arched back

Two pairs of spikes on its tail, known as a thagomizer

It had a very small **brain** that was about the size of a plum! It had the smallest brain of any dinosaur in proportion to its body size.

4.5 mph

Stegosaurus was an **herbivore** that ate low-growing plants, like moss and ferns.

It was a **quadruped** that walked very slowly on its four short legs, with a top speed of around 4.5 mph (7 kph).

STATS

Period: Jurassic (155–145 MYA)

Diet: Plants

Height: About 9–14 ft (3–4 m)

Length: Up to around 30 ft (9 m)

Weight: About 10,000 lbs (4,500 kg)

STEGOSAURUS

Cretaceous

BRACHIOSAURUS

BRAK-ee-uh-SORE-us

This dino was a huge **quadruped**, which means it walked on all four legs. However, it had longer front legs than back legs, which was unusual for a dinosaur!

Herds roaming!

In fact, the name **Brachiosaurus** means "arm lizard" for this very reason!

A back that sloped down toward the tail

Brachiosaurus had a **very, very long neck**, similar to that of a giraffe, but on a much bigger scale. This dinosaur was probably more than twice the height of a giraffe!

DISCOVERY

Year: 1900

Location: United States

By: Elmer S. Riggs, a paleontologist

Name: Means "arm lizard"

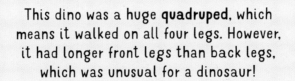

Triassic   Jurassic

This dino liked to snack on **leaves**, its **long neck** reaching high in trees!

52 spoon-shaped teeth for stripping plants, shoots, and leaves

As an **herbivore**, Brachiosaurus ate green things like plants—in other words, it was a **vegetarian**!

A large body to help it stay warm

It moved in groups, or **herds**, looking for food. It needed to eat **A LOT** of greens!

STATS

Period: Jurassic (155–140 MYA)

Diet: Plants

Height: Up to 40 ft (12 m)

Length: About 80 ft (25 m)

Weight: Up to around 80,000 lbs (36,000 kg)

BRACHIOSAURUS

Cretaceous

ARGENTINOSAURUS

ARE-jen-TEEN-uh-SORE-us

Argentinosaurus was one of the **largest dinosaurs** to have ever walked the Earth.

It laid eggs about the size of a **soccer ball!**

No one knows exactly how big it was because only parts of fossilized skeletons have ever been found.

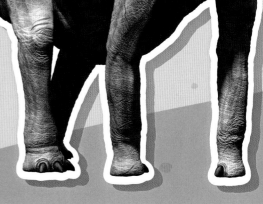

DISCOVERY

Year: 1987

Location: Argentina

By: Guillermo Heredia, a farmer

Name: Means "Argentine lizard" after its place of discovery

A long tail used for balance and defense

Triassic

Jurassic

This **giant** dino towered tall, with eggs as large as **soccer balls!**

A long neck to allow it to reach food without moving too much

Argentinosaurus was so big that predators such as **Giganotosaurus** (jig-an-OH-tuh-SORE-us) would have had to hunt it in packs, like wolves, to bring it down!

Argentinosaurus was an **herbivore** with a long neck and peg-like teeth for nibbling leaves.

Thick, sturdy legs to support its enormous body

STATS

Period: Cretaceous (90 MYA)

Diet: Plants

Height: About 70 ft (21 m)

Length: 100 ft or more (30 m)

Weight: Somewhere around 160,000 lbs (70,000 kg)

When these dinos moved in herds, you would definitely have heard them coming—the rumbling ground would have sounded like an **earthquake!**

EARTHQUAKE ZONE

ARGENTINOSAURUS

Cretaceous

TRICERATOPS

Try-SAIR-uh-tops

The name **Triceratops** means "three-horned face," because—you guessed it—it had **three horns!**

The two longest horns on its head were about 3 feet (1 m) long!

Watch out for horns!

A shorter, softer horn on its nose

hivore,

a
t

bar
cou   an

An enormous skull of around 7 fee~ (2 m) long

DISCOVERY

Year: 1887

Location: United States

By: O.C. Marsh, a paleontologist

Name: Means "three-horned face"

Triassic   Jurassic

A dino with a **great big head** and **horns** to fill T. rex with **dread!**

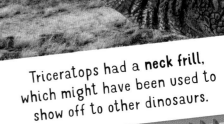

A **quadruped**, Triceratops could **charge** like a **rhinoceros** on all four legs, horns-first, to try to frighten off T. rex.

Triceratops had a **neck frill**, which might have been used to show off to other dinosaurs.

It had up to **800 teeth**. They wore down quickly, but this dino could easily grow more!

STATS

Period: Cretaceous (68–66 MYA)

Diet: Plants

Height: About 10 ft (3 m)

Length: Around 30 ft (9 m)

Weight: Around 12,000 lbs (5,500 kg)

It also used its horns to fight other Triceratops, just like male deer (stags) do.

TRICERATOPS

Cretaceous

TYRANNOSAURUS

tie-RAN-uh-SORE-us

T. rex was one of the most **fearsome** and **aggressive** dinosaurs!

You guessed it! This dinosaur was a meat-eater.

It had around **60 razor-sharp teeth**, each of which could grow to be as long as a banana!

DISCOVERY

Year: 1902

Location: United States

By: Barnum Brown, a fossil hunter

Name: Means "tyrant lizard"

Powerful jaws—4 feet (1.2 m) long—could easily crunch through bone.

In fact, Tyrannosaurus's bite was at least three times more **powerful** than that of a lion.

TYRANNOSAURUS

Along with **sharp** and **grasping** claws, this carnivore had awesome **jaws!**

The word rex means king, and **Tyrannosaurus** means "tyrant lizard." T. rex was the king of the tyrant lizards!

A tail for balance

Strong legs for chasing prey

Long, sharp claws

It was a **biped**, with muscular back legs and small but powerful arms.

T. rex had **binocular vision** and an excellent sense of smell.

Tyrannosaurus is often called **T. rex** for short.

STATS

Period: Cretaceous (68–66 MYA)

Diet: Meat

Height: Up to around 20 ft (6 m)

Length: About 40 ft (12 m)

Weight: Around 15,500 lbs (7,000 kg)

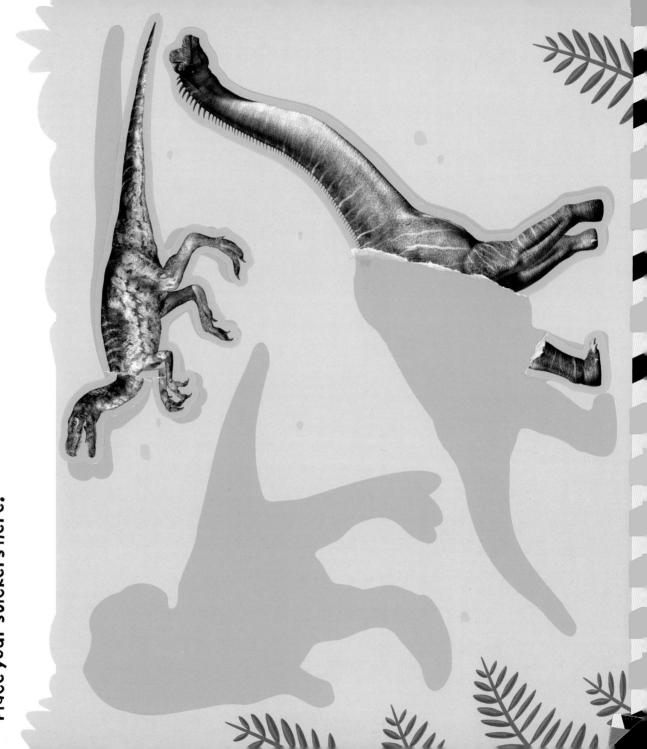

STICKER-SAURUS!

Place your stickers here.

WARNING! CARNIVORE ABOUT!